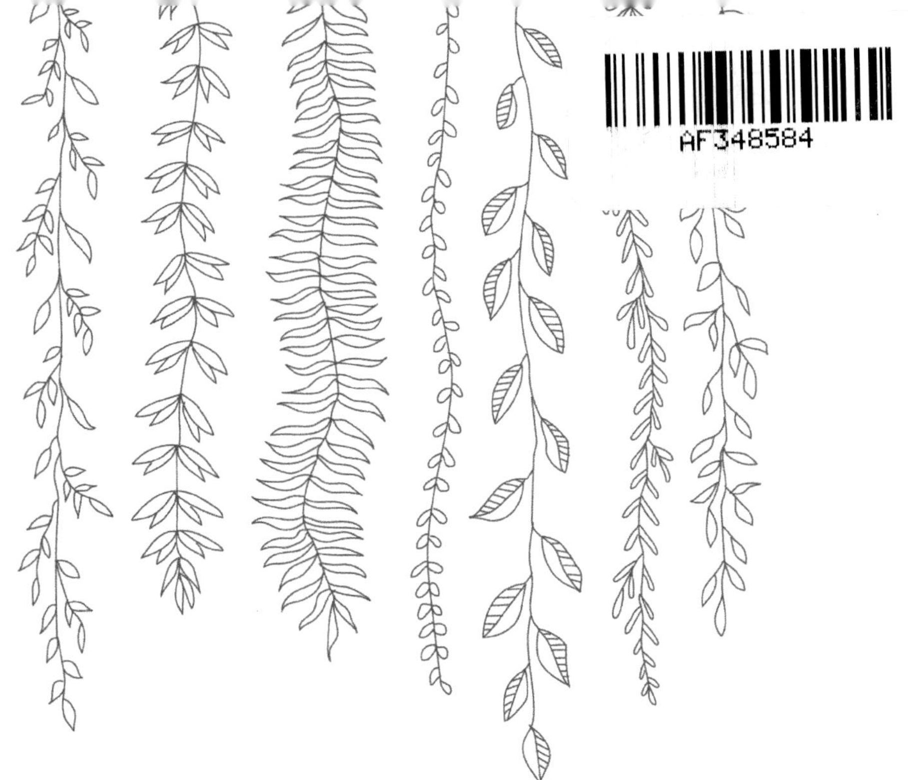

flourishing

A COLLECTION OF POEMS

BY SINA STEELE OF
her mustard faith

Published by Her Mustard Faith
Gordonton, New Zealand
www.hermustardfaith.com

© Copyright 2021 Sina Steele. All rights reserved.

First published 2021
ISBN Softcover 978-0-473-59819-8
ISBN Softcover POD 978-0-473-59820-4
ISBN EPub 978-0-473-59821-1

No portion of this book may be reproduced, stored in a retrieval system or transmitted in any form or by any means "electronic, mechanical, photocopy, recording or otherwise" except for brief quotations in printed reviews of promotion, without prior written permission from the author.

Cover design, illustrations and poetry body font by Sina Steele.

Cataloguing in Publishing Data
Title: Flourishing: A Collection of Poems
Author: Sina Steele
Subjects: Poetry, Christian life, Spirituality

A copy of this title is held at the National Library of New Zealand.

flourishing

A COLLECTION OF POEMS

BY SINA STEELE OF

her mustard faith

Endorsements

When I read Sina's words, it's almost like she knows my thoughts and prayers. This beautiful book of poetry tenderly ushers me back to the heart of the Father and makes me feel less alone. It's like sitting on my front porch with a friend who knows my soul.
—Lauren Eberspacher, Author of *Midnight Lullabies-Moments of Peace for Moms*, and the blog *From Blacktop to Dirt Road*.

I couldn't put this collection down. Sina's words are honest and raw, weaving together hope and light in a way that left me encouraged and inspired. *Flourishing* is a book you'll come back to time and time again. A faith-centered must-read.
—Liz Mannegren, Author of *Embrace*

Visually stunning, every page of poetry in this life-affirming collection points toward God's perfect love and constant presence like a balm to the struggling soul. *Flourishing* is an artistic masterpiece!
—Mikala Albertson, Author of *Ordinary on Purpose: Surrendering Perfect and Discovering Beauty Amid the Rubble*

Sina's book *Flourishing* is a brave share of personal struggles and courageous overcoming that will inspire and encourage all. Beautifully illustrated, this book features powerful reflections of healthy thinking that will lead you to a more truthful understanding of who you are and how much you are loved by your Heavenly Father.
—Janene Forlong, Author of *Where Fear Rules* and *Coming Home*

Everything about this book is beautiful visually, but also—it was like sitting down with an exceptionally wise and kind friend. You're going to love it.
—Stevie Swift, Author of *Bring Them Home* and *Capturing Thoughts*

Sina Steele's beautiful book *Flourishing* will captivate your heart and soul as she takes you on a life-giving journey through her poems. Her storytelling and relatable style will lead you into a deeper connection with God and yourself.
—Amber Palmer, Writer at *My Jars of Clay*

Sina's poetry reminds me of pages from a modern day Book of Psalms. She is able to express with words what others are feeling but unable to articulate. Her words are simply stunning.
—Natasha Smith, Writer at *Lovely You Blog*

Dedicated to my daughters, the wildflowers flourishing before my eyes.
I pray this book serves as a reminder that you can do the things the
Lord puts on your hearts. You are beautiful, brave, and kind—and being
your mama is a great privilege. Wherever you find yourselves in life,
I hope you always have the courage to simply flourish.

—Mama

Wildflowers

I've never thought of myself
As a wildflower
I more preferred the metaphor
Of a wallflower
Fading into the background
Only blooming as much
As a girl like me "should"
Minimising myself
So as not to offend anyone

Yet as the seasons roll on by
I sense this new affinity
With the wild ones—
The ones who grow
Unnoticed, unintended, undeterred
Their beauty is understated
Almost unnoticeable
Unless you're looking for it
Their beauty is not according
To traditional standards
It's an unfiltered rawness
That can't be confined to a curated newsfeed
It's in their resilience
The way they care not
To jostle for their place
Or compare their petals
To all the other flourishing florals

They simply fix their gaze towards the Sun
And bloom.

Don't give me conventional beauty
It's too predictable, too safe
Give me the beauty of a buttercup
Who cares not for the opinion of man
Give me the understated daisy
Who will spring up with grace
Even when you mow her down
To keep up appearances
Give me the wildflower
That grows on the roadside
Unruly, uninhibited, uncaring
Absolutely unaware
That others have an opinion of her blooming

Here's to the wildflowers,
A note to myself and the ones I'm raising—
Wherever you find yourself,
I hope you always have the courage
To simply bloom.

Note to self:
Wherever you find yourself,
I hope you always have the
courage to simply bloom.

Grace for the back roads

I used to carry
A sense of shame
For all the twists and turns
I've traveled along the way.
It always seems to
Take me a little longer
Than those around me.
But now, gratitude is my portion.
Now—
I have grace for the back roads,
The detours, the sidetracks,
The challenging adventures
Along the way.
I may be a little more
Beaten up, weathered,
Dirt smudged around the edges,
Have a little more
Battle scars to show my waywardness
Than those whose path
Has been smooth sailing.
But now,
Gratitude is my portion.

Now, I have grace for the back roads,
For they've led me here, back to You.

Brave, full stop

I keep writing then deleting,
Creating then erasing,
Stepping forward then stepping back,
Being brave then letting fear win.

Oh Lord, help me to be a woman who rejects hesitation.
I don't want my fears and insecurities
To hold me back from simply showing up.

Let me write,
Because I've entrusted the pen to You.
Let me create, because I recognize
You're the ultimate Creator.
Let me step forward
And not even consider stepping back.

Let me be brave, full stop.

Oh Lord, let Your voice silence those silly fears.

Lord, make me brave.

I'm wrestling

I'm wrestling,
Struggling,
Questioning,
Wandering,
Wondering,
Exhaling,
Thinking,
Pondering,
Imagining,
Revising,
Revisiting,
Respiring,
Destroying,
Discovering.

I'm wrestling with so much
Of this thing called life.
So many questions,
Leading to more questions,
And few answers.
The only thing that's certain,
Unchanging,
Unmoving,
Unquestionable,
Is You.

Undo all of me

I lay it all down at Your feet.

All of it. All of me.
Unclench these hands.
Uncallous this heart.
Unstick these feet.
Unravel this mind.
Undo this soul.

I lay it all down.
All I have and
All I am
Belongs to You.

Less of me please

Humble me
Cast me down—not for my crushing
But simply so You may become more
Less of me, more of You

Carve out the nooks where the darkness lurks
Until the hidden spaces are all laid bare
Then fill them up, shine Your light
Fall afresh, make me new

Let every edge be softened by the Potter's hands
The rough places smoothed
To be a place that others can rest
A place to lay down their load
Unshoulder the burdens that trouble their soul

Let the softened peaks and quiet curves
Of this subdued volcano
Shout the greatness of a King
Who gently sweeps the cobwebs and washes anew

Let the people come
Let the people say
She is different
She carries her world in a different way
She wears a crown not of this world
Her eyes are lifted when others are cast down
And let them know
It isn't really me at all

Less of me, more of You
Humble me so all they see is You

Write my story

You are writing my story.
I don't know exactly how
Everything will play out
And I don't know what bends and twists
Will appear along the way.
But I choose to relinquish the pen.
You are my author.

I trust You to write my story

My wandering heart

To my wandering heart:
Be fettered
Be bound
Be tethered
Be stuck onto
Be cleaved

You know not the depth of your wanderings,
The capabilities of your hostility—
You know the rage that burns,
A switch that turns
So quickly, too quickly—
You know the shame that follows.
You know the hurts you carry
The ones your countenance tries to hide
From others.

My wandering heart,
Bind yourself to Him.

He alone is good.
He is the good news for the world.
For the poor, the sick, the destitute,
The depressed, the desperate, the needy.

He is the good news for you.

Oh, wandering heart,
Bind yourself to Him.

Thoughts from today

You know all my doubts,
Every single hesitation
—And there's quite a few—
You know when my mind wanders
Far away from home.
You know my failings—
How well I know them, too.
So how can You still
Call me,
Choose me,
Want me,
Beckon me,
Love me?
How can You know my wanderings
And choose to put them in a bucket?
You bottle up my tears
And record them in Your book.
You see my failings yet choose to
Cast them into the sea
Of forgetfulness.
That leaves me undone.
All of it—
All of You—
Leaves me undone.

Closer to heaven

Sweet and gentle rolling hills,
You've captured me.
Captivated me.
Countless times I've meandered your fields—
From the luxury of my car—of course.
And I don't know how,
But your beauty seems to grow grander
As mine digresses.
Time favours your slopes
And curves and crevices—
How I wish the same
Were true for me.
Your beauty grows,
Deeper still, with each new season.
Sometimes I wonder if that's true,
Or if it's just my perception,
Fragments of wisdom,
Or something akin,
Added in as I age.
Either way—
Your mere appearance
Draws me closer to heaven itself.
A sense of awe
Washes over me
When I take you in.
I drink you up with my eyes
And exhale peace.
Oh, sweet and gentle rolling hills
You draw me closer to heaven itself.

Mere appearances

The lines are setting in,
Time will not favour
My curves for much longer.
The creases around my eyes
Chisel deeper each day.
The outside is aging,
Yet there's such a grace to be found.
An acceptance of the years
And tears and memories and laughs and sorrows
That have brought me here.
How sad it would be
If all I had to offer
Was held in a few quick flutters of the eye
And contoured skin.
Thank You God for a life
That is so much more than mere appearances.

. . . your beauty seems to grow grander
as mine digresses. Time favours your
slopes and curves and crevices—
how I wish the same were true for me.

Flourishing

And then one day,
she let go of all the things she never could control anyway.
And she simply began to flourish.

Flourishing—
An awkward, unusual phenomenon
When you're accustomed
To being a wallflower.
All the days of your life,
People have passed you by,
I don't berate them—
Why would they acknowledge a wallflower?
Simply part of the furniture.
Nothing to write home about.
Nothing to see here.
Move on.

Yet, everyone forgets—
Or at least I do,
That the seed grows in the utter darkness.
In the depths of the soil,
Unseen, unnoticed, undeterred.

And so it was with her.
The soil was fertile
And the time was right.
The people continued to pass her by.
Nothing to see here,
Nothing of note—
And she quietly, simply
Flourished.

Behold this woman

Her faith was leading her.
You could see it in her steps.
You could see it in her eyes.
You could see it in her words.
In fact, as you began to study her,
You could see it spilling over
From every nook and every cranny.
You started to realize
You were beholding a woman
Who had been changed to her very core.

I linger here

I wrestle with the world.
With my own flesh.
My wavering mind,
My fickle heart.
I say no to the busy,
The hurried,
The hustle.

I linger here,
A little longer than those around me.
I still myself.
I wait.
I just want to be
In Your presence.

Lord, unrush me.
Undo me.
Unhasten me.

Unravel the anxious thoughts,
Until my mind
Runs a straight line to You.

Go ahead of me.
Where You lead, I want to follow.
I just want to be
In Your presence.

So here I'll linger,
Just a little longer.

Every part of me

You know me.
Every outline,
Every curve,
Every nook,
Every cranny,
Every hair,
Every breath,
Every word,
Every thought,
Every step,
Every fear,
Every failure,
Every shame,
Every scar,
Everything.
Every part of me.
And You still care.
You still call me friend.

Lead me home

As I get older, I have this inward sense
Of shedding the layers that once enrobed me.

I find myself caring less about what others may think,
Though the insecurities still visit me often.
Intentionally peeling away familiar coverings—
Scary. Vulnerable. Exposing.

My mind is juxtaposed with turbulent thoughts—
The new thoughts pushing me to leave the worries behind
Yet the old mindset clinging on for dear life.

I wrestle with the truth that though
I desire to live with a renewed mind,
My old foes visit me often.
Fear, insecurity, worry, anxiety, anger—
Though I ache to abandon them completely,
They still find a home inside my head.

I try and fail and try and fail.
I am faced with the truth that was told from the beginning of
time: My fickle heart betrays me.

I bow my head.
The tears escape me and flow freely;
I let them run their course.
The tears once hidden no longer shame me,
For I know they do me good.

They lead me home to You.

My Potter

Lord, I've seen Your hand transform
The nooks and crannies of my soul.
Oh, sometimes I wish the work would
Be quicker but Lord, we both know
I'm forever a work in progress.

Let me be a willing vessel:
Moldable,
Teachable,
Patient on the days it hurts.
And oh how the pain
Scourges deep at times.
But let me always have
The humility to say:
You are my Potter
And I am the clay.

Her bravery

She's brave
And fierce
And determined.
But not in the way
You'd think.
She's not brave
Like a lioness
Or a tiger.
She's brave
Like a wildflower.
A lonely, forgotten,
Overlooked,
Unwanted
Wildflower.
Her bravery comes
From knowing her worth
In a world that wants
Her voice to be silenced.
Her bravery comes
From knowing she was
Woven together
By a King
Who calls her royalty
Even if the world
Wants to tell her
She's a weed.
She's brave
And fierce
And determined.
But not in the way you'd think.
She's brave
Because she knows her King.

Beauty from ashes

You make beauty from ashes.
You give joy where once there was mourning.
You shine light where once there was darkness.

You take broken hearts, shattered dreams,
The forgotten parts of our story—
And You offer redemption.

In the midst of the process,
I take courage.
I won't lose heart
For I know
You haven't
Finished with me
Yet.

Undo me

I'm learning to be still and wait on You.
How hard it is, but oh so necessary.
Lord, don't let me rush on ahead of where You're leading me.
I don't want normal, whatever that means.
I don't want an overwhelmed schedule
That leaves an underwhelming amount of time for You.
I don't want to spend my days hustling.

Lord, please.
Unhurry me.
Unrush me.
Undo me.
Unravel me.
Unhasten me.

Let me be a woman
Absolutely
Indelibly
Undeniably
Undone by You.

Lord, I want more of You.

My unlovely pieces

I've spent my days wishing away
So many pieces of myself.
Longing for less of this
And more of that.
Feeling broken in so many
Unseen ways.

But God,
You've gathered up
All my broken and unlovely pieces
And shown Yourself to be a
God of restoration.

What is broken, You restore.
What is unlovely, somehow,
You make lovely.

Beauty in the process

There's so much beauty in the process.
Sometimes it doesn't seem that way,
Because, how could there be beauty in pain?
But somehow, there is.
There is beauty in the cocoon.
There is beauty in the labour.
There is beauty in the burial of the seed.
The pain in the process is a precursor to newness.
Look at the butterfly that emerges,
The baby that is born,
The tree that grows.

Sometimes we want to
Skip over the process
Because it's so hard,
But God, I know You're working.
You will use this pain,
This writhing, searing pain,
I know You will.

Already, I see myself emerging
Stronger, more tenacious, more determined,
More resilient, and more beautiful,
Than ever before.

Cracked

The glass is cracked
Yet the light still seeps in—
In fact, because of all the cracks,
The warmth seeps in too.

—My life

There's so much beauty in the process.
Sometimes it doesn't seem that way,
Because, how could there be beauty in pain?
But somehow, there is.

The gentle dawn

I don't know exactly when it happened,
When the encompassing darkness
Yielded to the light of day.
All I know is I was driving along
With my high beams on and somewhere—
My memory fails me now—
I realised the gentle dawn
Hemmed me in.
Somewhere, somehow,
The light seeped in.
It didn't announce itself or demand attention.
Just a simple, unpretentious appearance
In the crossover between
Five and six am.
And I couldn't help but think
About all the moments in life
When the arduous has bowed to
The less hard.
And it doesn't assert itself,
It just arrives, so softly.
One day I look back and realise
The wound has faded to a scab,
And then, to a scar.
Oh the stories my scars could tell—
Stories of the night surrendering,
With a skillful reticence,
To the light of day.
I don't know how it happens
But the light of day
Always shows up,
At the right time.

Paradox of believing

The trees were more glorious,
The sun more bright,
The birds more chirpy,
The flowers more beautiful,
The grass more green.

And me, I was still the same,
Yet, somehow,
Totally changed.

—The paradox of believing

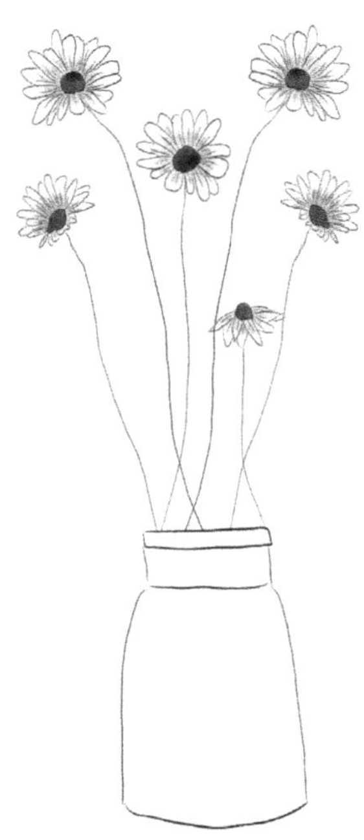

Let me praise Thee

As the days and months and years roll on by,
My heart is confronted by this inescapable reality:
Today is fleeting and tomorrow is no guarantee.

So, as long as I have breath in these lungs,
Let me praise Thee.

Oh, let me Praise Thee.
When the sun sneaks over my fence,
When the haeta gives way to this breaking day,
When the moon suspends itself expertly in the sky,
When the tui sings me a lullaby—
At least, I swear it was for me—
Those notes hit into the depths of my soul.
When the sun is scorching,
When the rain is pouring,
When the living is easy,
Or when sorrow sets in.
Whether the leaves
Are clinging to their branches,
Or in the process of letting go.
Whatever the season,
Whatever the occasion,
Whatever, whenever, wherever,
Oh my Lord,
Let me praise Thee.

As long as I have breath in these lungs,
Let me praise Thee.

Be still

In the quiet, still place,
There He meets me.

Be still, my soul.
Be still, my fickle heart.
Be still, my anxious mind.

Be still, and know—
He is God.

Dear 7 year old me

I'd tell her
She's loved,
She's beautiful,
She's smart,
She's worthy,
She's enough.

I'd tell her she'll grow up and do the things—
The ones burning on her heart.
But I'd warn her it'd take years,
And she'd have to work through
A heart ravaged by fear—
But she'd do it.

I'd tell her she would stumble along some windy roads,
With little encouragement along the way.
I'd tell her she'd want to give up,
Run away from it all—
But I'd tell her to stay the course.
Do the hard thing.
Be brave.

I'd tell her she'd need grace for the back roads
And patience for the scenic route,
And one day she'll look back and marvel at it all.
She'll trace His hand in it all,
Even the detours.

I'd tell her I'm so proud of her.
She's everything I hoped for and more.

Lift These weary arms

I'll lift my arms in praise,
Even when they grow weary.
I'll be a people of Your presence,
Even if I'm standing alone.
My lips will always praise You,
Even on the days they have no song.
My soul will give You thanks,
Even on the days it feels crushed.

Even though I'll fail You over
And over
And over again,
I'll always rise and praise You.

Undress my anxieties

You undress my anxieties.
All my disquieted thoughts
Are exposed in Your presence.
You arrest the thoughts
That have arrested my soul—
You know it's so hard for me
To let them go.
But You want so much more for me
Than imprisonment in my own head.

Gather them all up,
Send them on their way,
Even when it hurts—
Chaos never leaves without a fight.
I'm tattered and bruised
And weary from a lifetime of hurt.
But now, I'm waving a white flag in surrender.
I'm yielding to You.

The anxious thoughts—
I surrender them to You.
You dismantle them
Ever so tenderly,
Yet with unrelenting force.
You replace them with truth
And clothe me with Your peace.

You are still good

You are good
Even when I am not.
Even when life is not.
Even when the sun doesn't shine
And the children don't behave
And health and wealth fail.
Even when friends betray
And life disappoints
And the years thunder by too quickly.
Even then—
You are still good.

Here's what I'd say

If I could write a poem
To show you He exists,
To show you He is creative—

Then I'd tell you that you can see it in
The strength and majesty of the mighty kauri,
The lullaby of the tui,
The unfurling of the punga,
The yellow hues of the kōwhai tree.

I'd tell you the evidence is in
The glistening of the paua shell,
The crashing surf of Raglan,
The rolling hills of the King Country,
The curves and bends of this motu.

But move on south and there's still more:
The majesty of The Remarkables,
The stunning views of Fox Glacier,
The ups and downs of the Tararua Ranges,
The bellowing winds of the capital.

It's all there, my friend.
If I could sum it up,
I'd tell you that
Creation is shouting His name,
All up and down
The length of
Aotearoa.

Still in awe

It's been awhile,
This faith is not new.
These rhythms and lingo
Roll easily off my tongue.
But I don't want it that way.
Don't let me get so accustomed to the motions
That I forget the awe
And excitement
And transformational heart change
That took place.
The way Your presence
Entered in
And I was never the same.
Truly, never the same.
Please, help me to
Never lose my sense of wonder.
Still in awe,
Let me ever be.
Still in awe
Of You.

Always,
Ever in awe
Of You.

Her longings

She's voracious, and never quite satisfied.
She's hungry, but this world, it's so unfulfilling.
She's weary with a weariness that aches in her bones.
The days wear her thin, she can't explain why.
The ache in her bones,
The sigh in her soul.

She longs for more.

She longs for home.

She longs for more.
She longs for more.
She longs for home.

Flourish

The preacher man told me
I would flourish.
He just didn't say
It would be in small bursts
And that there would be so much pain
Along the way.
He wasn't wrong
But boy has it hurt.
Just to get a simple flaming bud
To push through the dirt.
He never said
How lonely it might be along the way,
That waiting in the dirt would feel so dark
And cold
And nothing at all like flourishing.

At least I don't think he mentioned that.
Or if he did,
I desperately didn't want to hear it.
I wanted to flourish
But without the pain,
Until I realised they were interlinked—
They were one and the same.

Hello God

Hello God,
It's me again.
I come to You to worship,
But how quickly my mind wanders.
How fickle the tendencies
Of my heart and soul.

I have so much to say
But, please, help me to listen.
Help the words of my mouth to be few—
The internal words, too,
As I strive to listen to Your voice.

I sense Your presence most
Out here in this stillness.
It's quiet—
But for the singing of birds,
The quiet babble of the stream,
And the rustling of leaves.

Oh, I sense You here.
I see Your creative hand in all these details.

Every ripple and reflection,
Every stone smoothed over by the water,
Every tui bird that sings a lullaby overhead,
Every green fern and wildflower,
Every cloud that traverses the sky,
Every ray of light dancing in the branches.
Even the moss that I trample underfoot,
Each one of them sings Your praise.

Even this stream,
Dribbling and nigh-on-dry,
Sings to You in praise.

Whether in a season of flourishing
Or one of drought,
All of them sing Your praise.

So here I am, God—
I come to You in worship.
I bring all of me,
Wandering mind,
Fickle heart and all.
All that surrounds me
Sings out to You in praise—
And so will I.

Ode to Autumn

The leaves,
They're changing.
They don't even seem afraid.
So why am I?
I loved their green,
Their luscious green.
But I love the tints and tones
They're becoming, too.
The yellows
The golds
The burnt umbers
The ambers
The not-quite blood red—
Each stage, each hue
Carries an unequivocal beauty
That contends not with
The hue that precedes.
You'd think there would be
A deep melancholy
With the eternal disappearance
Of each stage, each hue.
But there's not.
Simple awareness meets
Sobering surrender,
Proving change is inevitable
Yet all can still be well.
Could it be—
Are these leaves teaching me,
That change
Can be beautiful, too?

Grace to walk in

I've spent my days tiptoeing around,
Minimising myself.
But the God dreams inside are too big to be silenced.

Time is running on out of here
And the winds are changing
And I don't want to spend my days holding back.
God, You are so much bigger than my fears.
You are so much greater than the limitations
I've heaped on my own shoulders.

Remind me of this, day after day.
And when I forget,
Give me grace to walk in
The things You've prepared for me.

The pain of pruning

Bravely,
She gave herself over
To a season of pruning.
She knew it would hurt—
She knew it would be like
Having parts of herself
Cut right off.
She knew the nerves would spasm
And she'd feel like
Her heart
Was shattering and
There would be a lot of pain
And goodbyes
To parts of her
She had clung to so tightly.
She knew that even parts she liked
Might have to go—
Flowers that had once
Hung so delicately,
Fragrances that once
Defined her days.
But she knew it was part of it all,
Part of the defining,
Part of the refining.
So she gave herself to the process,
Softly, gently,
Yet all at once.

The day I believed

It was as though
I was witnessing it all for the first time.
Through new eyes,
Where the world seemed
Somehow more enchanting
Than it ever had.
Yet my eyes hadn't changed—
I still needed glasses to drive
And my tear ducts still gave way too easily.
Each iris still sparkled
A radiant, clear brown,
Like the day I was born.
My eyes were still the same
Yet my perception had changed.
And because of that,
I suddenly had changed, too.

—The day I believed

Falling together

I've seen this pattern before.
It all seems to fall apart,
Before it all falls together.
I can't explain it,
It doesn't make sense.
Yet, somehow, this pattern
Regularly emerges.
Every last piece of my life
Seems to fall apart,
And I,
Hanging on by a thread,
Lament anew.
Lament seems to be my anthem,
Forgetting the way
You never fail to come through.
Will I ever learn?
Will I forever complain?
Will my legacy be my short-sightedness,
Forgetting Your rainbow after the rain?
It all falls apart
Before it all falls together.
You've got a mysterious way
Of working in my life,
And it unsettles me,
Discomforts me,
Jolts me, awakens me,
In a way—a pattern, I suppose—
That I needed all along.

Hungry for truth

We're a people of convenience.
We want it all and we want it now.
We plant the seed and we want to
Eat the fruit immediately.
We want patience but we don't want
To endure the situations that grow it.
We're hungry for tomorrow but we want it today.
We want the fertile soil
But we're too lazy
To cultivate the unyielding landscapes
Of our own hearts.

Oh God, help us to be a people
Who hunger for holiness and truth
Over convenience and compromise.
Help us to set our eyes on the unseen, the eternal.
Help us to fix our eyes on You.

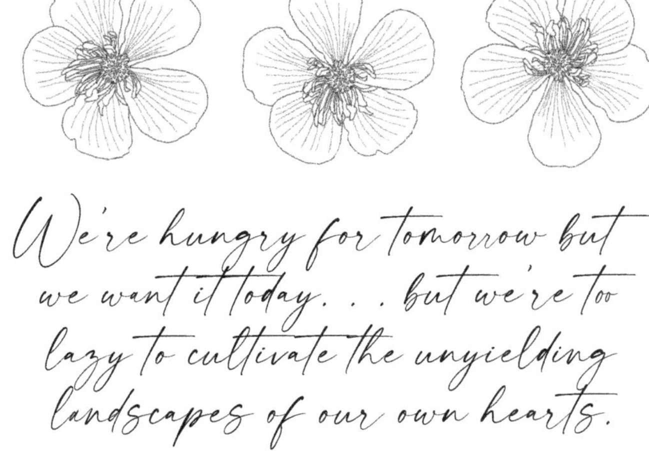

You fail me not

It's felt pretty dark this year.

Words have failed me, when so often, they've been my solace.
The pen guarding all its ink, safe for yet another day.
But Lord, my heart aches to spill over
The contents within.

As I pour out my heart before You,
Somehow, You make the light stream in
And shadows dance
In places where once the darkness lurked and reigned.

This year has been hard—so hard
And words fail me now
But You fail me not.

You've never failed me
And You will not begin now.
You've never failed me
Though I've certainly given You reason
To retreat.

Lord, this year has been hard
But please—
Let Your light continue to stream
Into the darkness.
Shine on my face once again
And let the shadows slip away.
This year has been hard—so hard
And words fail me now
But You fail me not.

You wreck me

You wreck me with Your goodness.
Sometimes, I think about
All the ways I've failed.
The messes I've made.
The parts of my story I wish
I could skip over.
But You—
You wreck me with Your goodness.
You know all the parts of me
I wish to forget
And You simply invite me to come,
Just as I am.
Oh Lord, You wreck me with
Your goodness.

Naivety

She didn't know,
At least at first.
She presumed the sun would stay faithful
And the gentle summer's breeze
Would forever warm her
Sun-kissed shoulders.
She thought the night
Would always arrive
With a final declaration
Of the sun's beauty.
But she didn't grasp
Harsh, unmelodious realities—
That breezes sometimes
Turn into tempestuous winds
And sunsets are sometimes
Obscured by menacing clouds.
And sometimes, there looms
An overwhelming darkness.
How little she knew,
Until life happened upon her.
The tempests and trials
Didn't dampen her hope.
Her faith weathered the storm,
But in turn weathered her—
She didn't know what she didn't know,
At least at first.

—Naivety.

I want to
be like water
Refreshing,
Cooling,
Life for parched lips.
I'll pour slowly
And slope my edges
To fit your expectations—
But I won't be more
Or any less
Than me.
If I'm too much for your vessel,
Or not enough,
So be it.
I'll swirl and play
And take up space
But I won't change who I am
For the sake of a mere man.
I'm water
And I'm finally accepting
Who He made me to be.

Simply bloom

Buttercups.
Ah, they just take my breath away.
I love the yellow jewels
That pop up on my field.
As I meander down my path,
They're there to greet me—
Humble, silent,
Yet screaming His glory.
They make no efforts to attract attention.
They don't want to be the star of the show.
They simply point their nose towards the sun,
And bloom.

How lovely would it be,
To do the same?
To turn my face towards the sun,
And simply bloom.

I think I'll do it.
I'll start today.
I don't want to be
The star of the show
Or force my way
To attention.
I just want to
Quietly, humbly
Shout His praise.

I think I'll do it today.
I'll point my face towards the Son
And simply bloom.

Morning thoughts

The morning sun hits
And it defrosts
My melancholy—
I can feel it in my bones.
I drink it up
With a tinge of sadness—
I'm not all the way thawed out yet.
There's crevices and crannies
Where the sun hasn't reached.
The scars that still ache
Upon even the
Gentlest caress.
The thoughts
That wage war against
What I know to be true.
But I won't dwell on them today.
I just want to sit,
And watch the sun
Chase the shadows away.
I long to hear Your voice
In this stunning silence.
I just want to linger here,
A little longer.
Pore over Your word slowly
And let it saturate me.
I sense Your presence here
In this morning dew.
And as I soak up every last
Piece of the flourishing warmth,
I think I could, quite happily,
All over again,
For the rest of my days,
Fall in love with You.

The faith I want

One that sticks around
No matter the weather—
No fair-weather fans here.
One that sings in the midst
Of the darkness,
A shaky lullaby
Even in the midst of sorrow.
One that is bright
When the world's darkness
Looms in and feels heavy.
One that troops on
Through weariness,
Through trials,
Through the seasons.
One that will not
Divorce my side,
No matter the situation.
This is the one I want.

—The kind of faith I want

Made for dancing

She's got a glistening in her eye.
There's a newness about her,
She doesn't even know why
But her soul wants to burst into dance

Wouldn't that make her look like a fool?

No matter, her soul was made for dancing.

Soul to soul

I wish we could talk more about
The things that fill our hearts.
About how it feels
To sit in God's presence
And explain to each other
What awe feels like
And how the Holy Spirit moves,
And how it's such a mystery.
I wish we could talk more about
All the unknowns
And the doubts and fears,
But how we have faith
Anyways.
I wish we could talk more about
Our imperfections
And outbursts
And wanderings and wonderings.
I wish we'd talk
About all the flaws we're ashamed of
And not shy away from hard
Conversations and altogether-too-exposing
Facets of our lives.
I wish we could talk
Soul to soul
Instead of always talking about the weather
And pretending as though
The chance of rain matters more
Than the scars that nearly broke us.
Let's talk about the real
And raw and hard and good—
I'm here for it.

Like I mean it

Let me praise
As though I really believe
The words I'm singing.
Don't give me religious motions—
I don't have time for games.
I'm here for the living waters
That my parched and desperate soul
Craves. Wants. Needs.
Fill me to overflowing.
Be balm for my heavy soul.
I'm here for the outpouring,
For the refreshing.
I'm wearing praise for You
Like an exquisite new dress.
I just don't have time
For nonsensical, empty religion.
I want to sing
Like I really mean it.

The seasons in me

The seasons come.
The seasons go.
And still I feel the same.
Can it be
That nature itself
Parades around us,
Coming and going,
Sowing and reaping,
Waking and sleeping,
Birthing and dying—
Yet I remain the same?
Or is it just
My short-sighted vision,
My heaven-forsaken apathy,
My refusal
To acknowledge
That the seasons
Are also for me?
The seasons come.
The seasons go.
And I can no longer cling to a pretense
Of firmly grasping to things
Beyond my control.
The season is coming—
She's here now—
To embrace truth.

Not wasting my todays

Lord, remind me that
Today is a gift.
I have woken up
With breath in these lungs
And life in these veins.
So, whatever troubles I may face today,
I choose to cling to Your Word,
Cleaving with all my being.

Don't let me waste my todays
Wishing for better tomorrows.
In the middle of my situation,
I will rise and praise You.

Note to self:
Don't waste your todays
wishing for better tomorrows.

You heard me

You heard my cry
Before it even escaped my lips.
A heart so heavy
With the burdens of yesterday.
Broken promises
And empty threats.
A heart so heavy,
It wondered,
Could I be worthy?
Could I be lovable
And able to pour out love,
Even as I am?
Even here—
In this space,
In this state,
In this way—
Could my heart be free?
Before the cry could even
Escape my lips,
You heard me.
You heard my heart
And that's when I knew—
I knew I could be free.

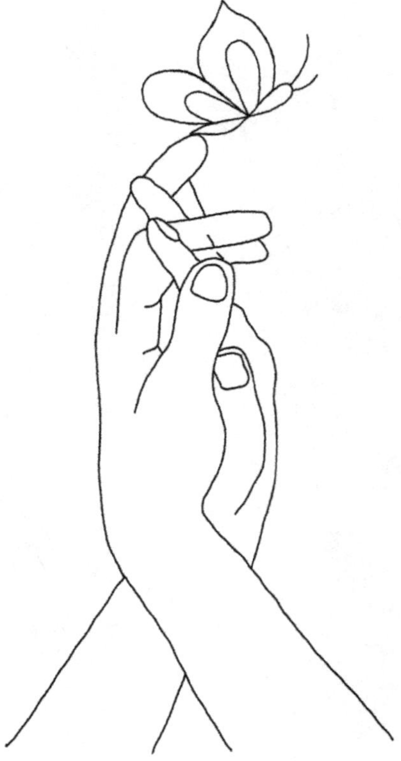

A collection of haiku

Her flowers faded
Though the spring blossomed outside
She was just so tired.

Stumbling in the dark
Suddenly a light pierced through
No longer alone.

Oh precious daisy
Your simple beauty astounds
Just bloom, daisy, bloom.

Sing me a new song
Oh sunset, show me your best
Display His goodness.

Let me linger here
In Your presence, at Your feet
I want to linger.

Sing me a new song
Use words, if necessary
Or, the sunset hues.

You've gathered me up

You've gathered me up.
All the unlovely bits
That have been lying in a
Covered, heaped pile in the corner.
I haven't wanted to touch it
Or known what to do with it.
I just wanted it to disappear,
Be gone.
But instead, it festered
And the shame grew.
I've looked at that heap,
Too many times.
It's become eerily familiar—
If it were to go,
I wouldn't know how to walk
On that side of the room anymore.
Is that why people don't change?
Because the old familiarity
Wields so much power
In a tired and weary heart?
This heap of unloveliness,
I don't even know where to start.
But You know;
You knew all along.
It didn't scare You,
Faze You,
Surprise You.
You've gently gathered me up,
All the unlovely bits
And carried me,
Temperamental heart
And all.

Leaning into You

I'm a sensitive woman.

Once upon a time,
This statement was a curse,
Or so it always seemed.
Too emotional, too teary—
That's what they said.
But they neglected so much,
Such short-sighted vision.

I'm a sensitive woman—
I now wear that without shame.
I'm sensitive to Your leading,
And I'm leaning into that.

I'm leaning into You.

You're water

You're water,
The kind I need.
But I've been full
Of so much for
So long,
I can barely
Handle what You have to offer.
I fear I may drown
At a few drops
Of Your goodness.
It's been so long
Since I knew the
Kindness of a stranger.
So please don't drown me
By pouring too quickly,
Or all at once.
Wade in gently,
I'm no longer afraid,
You're water,
And I need You.

Midnight believers

I want to sit with people who've
Sat at Your feet,
With people who've
Ventured through the fire
But don't care to spread their ashes
On passersby.
I want to sit with those who've
Endured pitch black nights
Yet still refuse to
Believe the darkness wins.
I want to sit with those who've
Tasted the shadows of death
Yet refuse to swallow bitterness.
I want to sit with people
Who've sat at Your feet.
Surround me with midnight believers—
The ones like Paul and Silas,
Who worshipped You
In the middle of the darkness,
Surrounded by prison walls.
I want people like this as companions—
And I want to be like this, too—
People who falter not in the night,
Unrelenting, unwavering, undeterred.
For I know You fail us not.
Let me be a midnight believer,
Sitting at Your feet,
Singing hymns to You,
Even in the dark.

Conversations in the car

I prayed today, in the car.
Except it was more just chatting.
Almost like to myself,
But in a friendlier tone,
And I realised that my journey
Has led me here—
To a place of conversations in the car,
Chatting into the wind,
Unafraid to expose my heart
To the One who already knows it all.

I used to be afraid—
Tiptoeing around,
Being sure to use the right phrases.
Adding in a few extra 'Father God' and 'Lords'
Just to be sure You knew
That it was You I was addressing
And not myself.
Or was it to make sure the crowd knew?
Now, I'm not so sure.
I'm not sure of a lot, actually.
The more I journey, the more certain I am
That I'm a desperate woman in need
Of a good God.
One who will answer
When my voice whispers faintly
Or natters away casually
In the car.
My journey has led me here—
Unafraid to expose my heart
To the One who already knows it all.

For me

Jesus, the One who
Calmed the storm
And the raging sea.

The One who loved the sinner,
The harlot,
The tax collector,
The most despised,
The least esteemed.

The One who
Washed the feet of His betrayer
And called him friend.

The One who looked out
On those who begged for Him
To be crucified and
Prayed for them
To be forgiven.

The One who died and rose again,
For the least of these.

For me.

Uprooting, again

Each year that passes
Seems to bring a new confusion,
A new questioning.
Almost like my feet
Are finally planted in
Firm soil,
Then uprooted once again
When my beliefs are challenged.
I'm not unhappy—
There's a strange comfort to be found
In the shaking and
Uprooting process.
Almost like the more it happens,
The more you're ready,
And the more you're ready,
The more uprooting comes.
I used to think
I'd be someone planted
For all my days
In the soil of my youth.
But now I see,
It's You.
It was You all along—
The Master Gardener,
Planting and uprooting,
Watering and pruning,
As You see fit.
So now, this process,
I trust it,
For I trust You.

Drive me to You

Falling in love
Or falling apart—
Both of these
Drive me to You.
Both spark a
Waterfall of words.
Sometimes it drowns me,
And sometimes it brings
The refreshing I need.

Enchanting sound waves

I heard a song
And it hearkened me back
To a season long gone.
How does this happen,
What magic is this?
That just a few sound waves
Could transport me back
To years ago when my skin was
Not yet fettered with lines
And the worries so minuscule.
I was taken back
To bonfires
And laughs,
New faith that was growing,
Excitement,
Flirting with my not-yet husband
Who was not-yet anything
As far as I was concerned.
Hearkened back—
Something about nostalgia
Gets me every time.
Just a few notes,
A few silly tunes,
And I'm young and free
Again.
How bittersweet you are,
Enchanting sound waves.

You are welcome

You're like water
To a thirsty soul.

And I'm a thirsty soul,
Searching for You.

Come on in.
The doors are wide open.
~~I'm anxious.~~
~~I'm fearful.~~
~~I'm not sure if I'm ready.~~
~~I'm not sure of so much.~~
Yet I'm thirsty.

You put my fears out to rest.
Come on in—
You are welcome in this place.

Help my unbelief

You crossed the ocean
Just for me.
But I was too afraid
To cross a puddle for You
In return.
You dragged that Cross
To Calvary.
You bled and died
Just for me.
So why am I like Peter
And hide in the shadows?
I tell everyone
I'm Your disciple,
But if I was confronted
In the public square,
Would I shout Your praise?
Or would I feel
Guilt and shame
When the cock crows thrice?
Help me, help my unbelief.
Help my voice to speak up,
Even if it's shaky.
Strengthen my arms,
So when the time comes
They'll be ready to swim.
Ready to cross an ocean
For You.
Ready to carry my cross
For You.

Have Your way

I say have Your way,
But sometimes,
The surrender is all too much.
I think You know my heart—
My heart so longs for Your will.
Come, Lord Jesus,
Have Your way—
Even on the days
My heart is faint.

Out of my box

I used to have You pinned down,
Put in a box.
A god who worked
Within the boundaries
I'd constructed.
I was so sure—
I guess because those I followed
Were so dogmatic—
Of how You operated.
The preacher man said
You did this and that
But never worked this way or that way.
So I believed him.
I had You figured out—
Or so I thought.
Turns out, years later,
I don't have much
Figured out at all.
All I know is I'm a dot,
A mere breath,
A passing shadow,
A wildflower that will soon wilt and die.
But You—
You're big and not a mere breath.
You're not a wildflower—
But You did create them.
And I'm starting to see
You won't fit in my box.
And for that, I'm grateful.
How naive I was to think any differently.

A woman marked

I want to be a woman
Marked by rest, not hurry.
By His presence,
Not my own ambition.
By peace, not striving.
By a listening ear,
Not a mouth that must be heard.

When others see me,
I want Him to be greater,
Me to be less.

More of Him, less of me.

Autumnal sunset

I saw the sunset yesterday.
I swear it was just me,
But the hues seemed
More sensational than usual.
As summer turns to fall,
The transition from sun to dusk
Is a little colder,
A little cooler,
And the sun seems to
Say goodbye
A little more beautifully.
As if to say—
Darling,
It's getting colder.
Frigid spells are looming
And the seasons are changing.
Harder times are coming—
There'll be fog and dew and chill
Abounding,
But there's still beauty to behold,
Right here.
Right now.
That's what the sunset seemed to say.

Make me usable

Temper me down
Condition me
Mold me
Soften me
Make me usable
In Your hands.
Let not the edges
Of my character
Be so tough
They can't be bent.
Let not my fickle heart
Expose itself too cracked.
Smooth me
Like the stream
Rolling over the stone—
Gently, painlessly,
Yet all at once.
Temper me down
Steady my soul
Make me usable
In Your hands.

You are the Potter

You are the Potter
And I am the clay
So why do I so desire
To shape my own way?
You soften me gently
But I hurry along—
The beat of my heart
Sings its own silly song
You give Yourself freely
And freely I take
Yet selfishness ruins me
Oh soul, come awake
Lay down all your plans
Give the Master His place
Yield your aspirations
And receive His sweet grace.
He's firing up the kiln
It's time to be refined.
He is the Potter
And I am the clay
It's time to yield
There's no time to delay.

How great Thou art

I just wanted to walk down
To my local coffee shop,
But the path
Was so busy
Declaring Your praise,
I got distracted immediately.

The way the sun caught the
Autumn leaves—
I don't know why,
But the beauty of it
Made me want to cry.
The way the wildflowers
Glistened so quietly
And the trees swayed
In the gentle breeze,
As if they were
Dancing to a song
No human has ever had the privilege
Of hearing.

I don't know why,
But the beauty of it all
Gets me,
Deeply,
Every time.

Oh Lord, how great Thou art!

Oh whenua

Here's to the barren places,
The streams running dry,
The overgrown banks
And mangled wildflowers.
Who forgot you my friend?
Did it happen somewhere
In the change of seasons?
Or when the haeta gave way
To the rising sun?
Were you forgotten in the daylight
Or the cover of night?
Oh, pō marie!
Was it the daytime that betrayed you—
Or simply the history books
That forgot to stamp your name,
Your significance?
Well, this is an ode to you,
My beautiful whenua.
I know you don't belong to me,
But I took my first breath on your shores
And so I belong to you.
If the daytime forgot you,
Let me not copy her ignorance.
If the nighttime betrayed you,
Let me shame her on your behalf.
Oh whenua, you have been trampled,
Ruined and left for dead.
They say it's always darkest right before the dawn.
Well, it's been dark.
It's time for dawning.
It's time for day.
My whenua, you shall have your day.

Feelings

You gave me the wrong directions,
Time and time again.
You're so strong—
Forceful—
And I follow you along,
To my own detriment.

You've wounded me,
Put me in situations
I couldn't back out of,
Forced me into confrontations
That dug me deeper
Into a trench of unloveliness.

You're not always bad—
I know you can be good,
So good.
Yet you never
Want to follow.
Can't you let truth
Be the leader?

You've given me the wrong directions
And wound me up at
Regret's door.
I know you can be good,
If only you would get in line.

—Thoughts on feelings

A new season

Sometimes,
My heart feels like it could,
Quite simply,
Altogether shatter.

A new season—
An exciting hello
Tinged with a mournful goodbye.
Goodbye to places,
To people,
To memories
That have woven themselves
So deep in my being
That saying goodbye
Feels like peeling off
A layer of myself—
Painful, heart-wrenching,
Unpleasant.

But now the time has come.
The necessity makes it
No less of a traumatic ripping
Of my flesh.

But I yield to the new season,
I usher it in with
All of me that remains.
And to some of you I say goodbye,
Though my heart shatters—
Thank you for every yesterday
Along the way.

Here in the middle

You meet me,
Right here in the middle.
I don't know what's up ahead,
So go with me.

Lead me, guide me,
Bind my fickle heart to Yours.
Tether the strings of my heart to Yours.
Where You go,
I want to go.
Where You lead,
I want to follow.

I'll sing Your praise

When the lights are shining
And the crowds are pressed all around
When the people are singing in unison

I, too, will sing Your praise.

When the crowds disperse in droves
And none gather to give You praise
No hushed whisper of Your name in the air

I, alone, will sing Your praise.

When the rising sun is beaming
And cracks of light trickle down to my soul
The warmth cradling my fickle heart

I, standing tall, will sing Your praise.

When the darkness gathers quickly
And the warmth of day flees for cover
The shadows taunting my anxious mind

I, knelt in prayer, will sing Your praise.

When the mountain is conquered
And panoramic views fill my gaze
The satisfaction of reaching the summit

I, victorious, will sing Your praise.

When the valley depths surround me
And the pit feels like my home
The cold and wind adorn me

I, in anguish, will sing Your praise

When the light of day is breaking
Or the dark of night is beckoning

When the cry of new life invades
Or the lamentations of death blow in

When loved ones cleave with endurance
Or closest friends divorce my side

When my body is flourishing and robust
Or disease wreaks havoc within

Through it all—

After it all—

In spite of it all—

I will always sing Your praise.

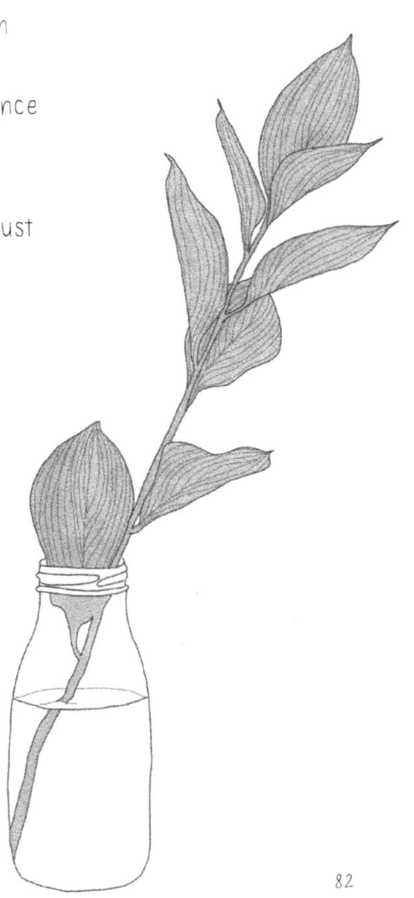

Pining for the Cross

Maybe it's the angst I feel inside,
Maybe it's the chaos in the streets,
Maybe it's the state the world is in,
Maybe it's just where I'm at in my own personal journey.

But I've been thinking about the cross a lot lately.

Along my garden path
Humbly sits a cross,
An old, rugged cross,
Reminding me of what my Jesus did—
For me.

And lately, as I walk that path,
I feel such a sense of wanting to lay at the foot of it.
To empty my mind of the worries
That so quickly find a home inside.
To lay my burdens down.
To brush off anxious thoughts and selfish ambition.
All the 'stuff'—
The weight of it all is so heavy to carry.

And then I think about how He carried it all—
It's overwhelming;
I find myself coming undone.
I lay all of me at the foot of the cross:
Your pain for mine.

May we find ourselves
A people at the foot of the Cross of Calvary—
Pining for home, pining for truth,
Pining for more of Him and less of me.

Tether my heart

Tether the strings of
My heart to Yours.

Though my fickle heart has a tendency
To sway with the breeze,
You are constant,
Unfailing,
Unchanging.

Though my feet sometimes trip
And stumble,
You reach down
And gently pick me up
And set me back
On Your path.

Eyes to see

You're in it all—
I know, I've got eyes to see.
There's no one single thing
That encapsulates all of who You are.
But there's flickers of You,
All over.

The sparkle in her eye
The blood-red of the autumn leaf
The dew sung in with the haeta
The daisy jewels adorning the field
The laughter of a child—
How I wish I could bottle that up.
The caress of a weary, weathered hand
That somehow warms my bones.
The swaying of the toetoe tussocks
As they gently whisper Your name.
The raging waves that kiss the shore
With tempestuous desire.

There's flickers of You
Everywhere.
I know, I've got eyes to see.

Wade out

Don't come looking
In the shallows.
If you want any part of me
You need to be prepared
To wade out into the deep.

I just want to go deeper.
Throw caution and the opinions
of others to the wind...
wade out with me into the deep.

Yearning for home

How do you begin to tell the stories
That live inside you
But you've never heard them uttered?
How can I say I feel the waves
Of Samoa rolling in my hips,
When I've never visited her shores?
How can I say I worship Him
With a language that feels foreign
Yet at the same time
Feels eerily like home?
A lullaby, a melody,
A swaying of the hips,
And I'm home.
How do I begin to own
The feelings and beatings of my
Own heart,
When the blood of two cultures
Flows within?
How? I don't know,
But I sense this longing
For a home I've never known.
I suppose this is what C. S. Lewis meant
When he said our yearnings
Were for our forever home.
Not this side of heaven,
But for heaven itself.
All I know is I feel it strongly,
A heart connection.
A desire, a tug, a thirst
For a place I've never been.
I yearn for home.

My wanderings

You've taken account
Of all my wanderings—
Do they ever get
Too numerous?
Do they ever spill over
From the jar,
Unable to be contained?
I know the answer—
I'm never too much
I'm never not enough
For You.
So Lord,
Bind my wandering
Heart
To Thee.

This journey

This journey—
I'm learning
So much about You
And so much about me.
The parts of me I always
Wished away,
The culture I left at the door,
The nooks and crannies of my soul
That seemed so ill-fitting—
I longed to displace
And forget them.
But how can you
Lose a piece
Of your own heart
And not walk around,
Incomplete?
Now,
This journey—
I'm learning
You complete me, but You
Don't just leave me be.
You beckon me come
And in the process,
Hand back to me
The pieces I tried to
Leave behind.
You're taking my brokenness
And making me whole.

The art of Kintsugi

I love the
Japanese art of Kintsugi.
Golden repair.
How beautiful to think
That broken pottery can be repaired,
Woven back together
With gold—
Instead of hiding away
My brokenness,
I am welcome to bring it
And let precious gold
Fill in the cracks and gaps
And nooks and crannies
And make me whole,
Make me new.
I think God works
In our lives
Like kintsugi,
Weaving together
Our broken pieces
And making us new.
Beauty from brokenness.

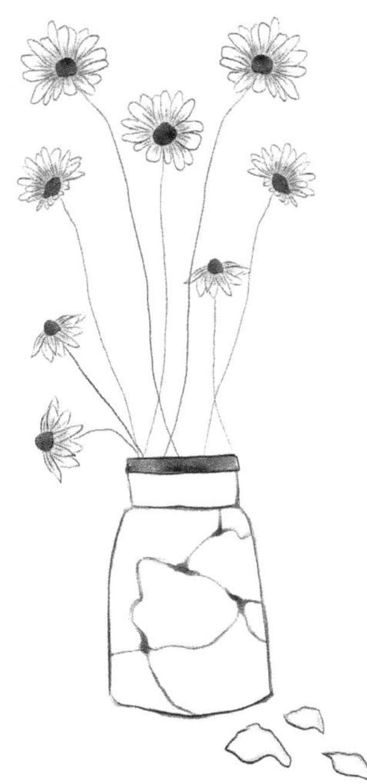

Lead me home

In every season of my life,
I turn to You.
I know You will
Make a way,
Even when there
Seems to be no way.

I take the fear
And worries
And anxieties
And troubles of my soul
And hand them over to You.

I trust You with my todays
And every single one of my tomorrows.

Lead me home to You.

Fluid and free

You're fluid
And free
And travel how You please.
You weave in and out
And do what seems
Like a little bit of magic.
You're a mystery—
Sometimes a tornado,
Sometimes a dove,
Sometimes like water,
Sometimes like fire.
I can't explain it
But You weave and leave
These little hints of miracles
And You never leave a place,
Or a person,
Unchanged.
I want to be fluid
And free,
And move with You.

—On the Holy Spirit

More haiku

I sense Your presence
In the trees, the leaves, the breeze.
Your Spirit abounds.

Kakariki green
I linger amongst the trees.
Flourish now, I pray.

Season overdue—
I waited but you came not.
So let's start anew.

Glancing at the floor
Lowly low until You came
Now I gaze on high

Gentle, little leaf
It is time to fall away
Let go without fear.

You call me friend

Thomas.
You just called him Thomas,
Your friend.
Not doubting Thomas,
Like we tend to call him.
You invited him in.
You invited him to
Touch your scars—
Did that hurt?
Did it hurt him,
To see his friend
Wounded so?
Truthfully, I'm just like him.
I have my doubts,
A wandering mind,
A fickle heart.
I want pretense to have no part of me—
You know my everything anyway.
And you don't call me
Doubting Sina,
You just call me friend.

His poiema

Your Word says I'm
Your masterpiece,
Your workmanship,
Your handicraft,
Your poiema.
Your fingerprints are all over my design.
But if I'm honest,
I haven't spent my days living that truth.
I've walked around head down,
In utter defeat.

You are the Master Poet,
The Artist,
The Creator.
Let my life be a reflection of Your very heart.
Let the poetry of my life be
A sweet fragrance to You.
Help me to walk in the good things
You have planned for me.

You are the Poet,
And I, Your poem.
I surrender to each stanza,
Every movement of the pen.
You dot my i's and cross my t's
You make me secure; You put me at ease.
You are the Master Poet,
And I, Your poiema.

The whisper of my soul

Not all ships make speedy voyages.
Sometimes, the sun sets
And the night seems far too long.
Sometimes, the seed tarries,
Abiding long in the darkness,
The deep darkness of the earth.
Lord, whether my journey
Is long or speedy...
Whether the haeta reaches me quickly
Or dawn delays...
Whether I flourish quickly
Or over many seasons...
Let me praise You
All the same.
The cry of my heart
And whisper of my soul
Is to always praise You.

Give me His presence

Don't give me hype
Or a quick fix.
I'm not looking for entertainment.
Time thunders by too quickly
To simply have my ears tickled.
Give me the presence of God,
Whether that comes slowly
Or all at once.
Don't give me empty religion—
I can no longer stomach the taste
Of an apathetic generation.
Give me the presence of God
Or nothing at all.

Daisies and buttercups

Look at the roses in bloom!
Their beauty is truly spectacular.
There's no questioning it.
An unopposed truth,
Visible from afar.
That's why they're chosen
To grace the hands of
Brides and their maids.
That's why they're chosen
For centrepieces and mantle places
And precious, expensive vases.
But, if I'm honest,
It's the plain old daisies
And buttercups
That take my breath away.
Their beauty is subtle, almost unnoticeable,
Whimsical and brave—
If you ask me.
They won't grace a
Bridal bouquet or sit at a wedding banquet.
But do you see
The way
They grace
Entire fields, effortlessly?
Their beauty is subtle
And oh so brave,
If you ask me.

Dancing with the Word

I know I'm inspired
When my hands can't keep up
With the words in my brain.
My handwriting, barely legible,
Scribbles so quickly
Across the page.
Lord, let this be
The story of all my days:
A woman who danced
With the Word Himself
On every page.

Falling in love

The sun shines
And sometimes, it scorches
An already cracked surface.
But sometimes,
It gently kisses
My weary forehead.
I lean into it
And I think I could,
Quite happily,
Fall in love with You
All over again.

Immerse me

How do you give
The ocean
To a woman
Afraid to get her feet wet?

Slowly but surely,
And then all at once.

Immerse me in Your presence.

It's time to fall

The seasons are changing,
And with them,
So am I.
Uncertain and unwilling,
At least at first.
It seemed scary—
Not right even—
To say there was goodness
In the goodbye.
But now, the leaves,
They're teaching me
That it's okay—
Necessary even—
To let go.
To fall.
To trust the process.
To say goodbye to things,
To time, to people,
To places, to seasons.
It's okay—
It's right even—
To embrace change.
The seasons are changing,
And with them,
So am I.

A deep well

A deep well of emotions
Churns within.
Sometimes I yearn
For the solace of the shallows.
Not for lack of depth
But simply to get a reprieve,
A rest, a reposing,
For an overworked mind
And an overwhelmed soul.

This deep well—
It contains so much of me.
A safe space to hide
All my hurts and failures,
Bitterness and rage.
I'm not reticent to
Expose my wanderings,
At least not anymore.
What would it profit me—
It's all out there on my sleeve
Anyway.
It's in the glances and furrows
And frowns and heavy sighs,
And the sparkles in my eyes.
I want pretense to have no part of me,
So I usher You in.

This deep and anguished well
Will praise You from within.

You're water

And I'm a parched soul
In a dry and thirsty land.
Fill me up,
Let me overflow.

Don't stop these words

The words
Can't stop—
Won't stop—
I don't want them to stop.
I don't want them to dry on up
And leave me here
Alone,
Empty,
Unable to express
The sentiments
That hide in the shadows.
I want to praise You
All my days,
And these words,
They help me to do that.
These words
Of praise,
Of awe,
Of thanksgiving—
I don't want them to stop,
For all my days.

You know me

You know me
With a depth that both
Frightens and comforts me
At the same time.
To intimate such a love
For such a fickle being—
I can't comprehend it,
Yet I can't live
Without it.
It's You:
You're the one
My soul loves.
You're the one
I both run to
And run away from,
Depending on the day.
I've known not the notion
Of pining for a mere creature,
Yet I know the
Longing for Your presence.
A familiar pang,
Bubbling beneath the surface.
You know me
With a depth
That frightens me,
Yet a depth I long for
With every fragment of my soul.
Take me deeper
Than the deepest waters.

Acknowledgements

I would like to thank my family and friends for their love, prayer, and support.
To Aaron—thank you for encouraging me to pursue the dreams on my heart,
and for being a great dad to our beautiful girls.

Thank you to Martin and Joyce for the way you have encouraged our family and
provided a safe space for us to flourish. Thank you to Zoe for your friendship
and for pushing me out of my comfort zone. Thank you to Ben for editing and
for helping me get this book to the finish line.

And finally, thank you, the reader. Thank you for taking the time to flick
through these pages. I pray you will be encouraged and inspired to turn your
eyes heavenward, and have the courage to flourish, wherever you find yourself
in life. Bless you.

Sina xx

Please get in touch;
I'd love to hear from you:
sina@hermustardfaith.com
www.hermustardfaith.com
FB: @hermustardfaith

www.ingramcontent.com/pod-product-compliance
Lightning Source LLC
Chambersburg PA
CBHW051348140126
38175CB00038B/795